ages 3 —

MW00993119

God Is Like a Mother Hen and Much, Much More

by Carolyn Stahl Bohler

illustrated by Dean Nicklas

with help from daughter Amy

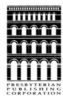

PRESBYTERIAN
PUBLISHING
CORPORATION

Published by Presbyterian Publishing Corporation
Louisville, Kentucky

Printed in Mexico

ISBN 1-57153-200-5

Dedicated to
Alexandra and Stephen Bohler,
who teach me about God

God is like a Mother Hen . . .

who protects her little chicks.

God is
like a
Caring
Daddy . . .

who listens really well.

God is
like a
Teacher . . .

who smiles and says, "Try again."

God is like

A Mother Hen,
A Caring Daddy,
A Smiling Teacher . . .

and
much,
much more.

God is like a Best Friend . . .

who plays and shares with you.

God is
like a
Mommy...

who kisses all your hurts.

God is like the Air . . .

right there, but you can't see it.

God is like

A Best Friend,
A Mommy kissing hurts,
the Air . . .

and
much,
much more.

God is like a Child . . .

who loves to have surprises.

God is
like You . . .

sometimes crying,
sometimes laughing.

God's Love is like a Teddy Bear's . . .

ready for snuggling at night.

God is like

A Child,
You,
A Teddy Bear's Love . . .

and
much,
much more.

Can YOU think of what else God is like?

God is like

A Mother Hen,
A Caring Daddy,
A Smiling Teacher,
A Best Friend,
A Mommy kissing hurts,

The Air you can't see,
A Child loving surprises,
You, crying or laughing,
A Teddy Bear's Love,
Sara,
and much,
much more.

Note to parents and smiling teachers:

We name God with metaphors. With each appropriate metaphor, we can say, "Yes, God *is* like that!" We can also say, "But in *some* ways, God is *not* like that!" Both responses are necessary, for God is not exactly like any of these metaphors; God is much, much more than any one.

The metaphors we use do not all need to be found in the Bible, yet our tradition does give valuable clues for how we might think of God. For some of the metaphors in this book there are numerous biblical references. Others are used only a few times. Some, like "Teacher," are alluded to by the way God is said to be acting, that is, like a teacher, teaching. I list here a citation or two for each metaphor.

Mother Hen: Matthew 23:37; Luke 13:34;
    Deuteronomy 32:11–12 (Eagle)
Daddy (Father): Luke 12:32; John 16:32
Teacher: Hosea 11:3; 1 Corinthians 2:13
Friend: Implied in Luke 11:5–6
Mommy: Isaiah 49:15
The Air (Breath): Genesis 2:7; Acts 17:25
The Child and You (the reader): Genesis 1:26–28
Love (steadfast love, experienced by a snuggling teddy bear):
    1 John 4:7–10, 16